NEWQUAY'S

PICTORIAL PAST

Compiled by

NEWQUAY OLD CORNWALL SOCIETY

First published 1983 by
NEWQUAY OLD CORNWALL SOCIETY

Second edition, revised, published 1993 by
LANDFALL PUBLICATIONS
Landfall, Penpol, Devoran, Truro, Cornwall TR3 6NW
Telephone: 0872-862581

© Newquay Old Cornwall Society

A CIP catalogue record for this book is available from the British Library.

ISBN 1 873443 08 0

Printed by the Troutbeck Press
and bound by R. Booth Ltd., Antron Hill, Mabe, Penryn, Cornwall

Cover photograph:
Boats of the Newlyn herring fleet leaving Newquay harbour, about 1900

NEWQUAY'S PICTORIAL PAST

When the idea of this book was first mooted, we decided that we would not attempt to write yet another history of Newquay. The following photographs were chosen from about 1,200 in the Woolf/Greenham collection. We hope that you, the reader, will enjoy our selection and that you will be stimulated to walk around Newquay and compare the "then" with the "now".

David Sharpe
Chairman,
Newquay Old Cornwall Society

The Local History Collection
of the Newquay Old Cornwall Society

GALLERY OF OLD NEWQUAY

on display at Chapel Hill, Newquay, off Central Square

A rapidly changing town like Newquay should not lose sight of its fascinating past. Members of the Newquay Old Cornwall Society have been collecting memorabilia and artifacts representing the history of Newquay and the surrounding area for many years and are doing so today. We wish to share our local history with you. The Society is a registered charity and raises all funding to manage, supervise and display the collection by donations and members' activities. The beautifully renovated premises housing our collection since Easter 1988 are generously provided by local businessman Mr Eddie Kowalski.

EVERYONE IS WELCOME.

Opening times vary according to season. Parties by arrangement.
There is an entrance fee.

Today, the town of Newquay is rightly regarded as a modern 20th century holiday resort yet it has a history which goes back 5,000 years. In written records it is first mentioned in 1305 when it is given the name TEWYNPLUSTRI (Cornish: towan = sandhill, lystry = boats, which makes "boats cove in the sandhills"). Much of the west part of the town is built on those sandhills. The name became Anglicised to Towan Blystra, a name which can be seen perpetuated on some buildings in the town. However, in 1439, Bishop Lacey of Exeter granted an indulgence for the building here of "a new keye for the rode of shipping". Thus commenced its modern name as two words New Key which has ended as we see it today NEWQUAY.

Those who visit Newquay at the height of the summer season may not be able to capture the full beauty of this lovely area. Fortunately, though, a vast number of our holidaymakers come to us in the spring, early summer and the autumn when we are at our best. They adore the unrivalled natural beauty - the light, colour, superb cliff-top setting, beaches and surf. Many are of an enquiring mind and see things they would like to know more about. Whenever they come, it is for them the following notes have been written.

Charles Woolf
President,
Newquay Old Cornwall Society

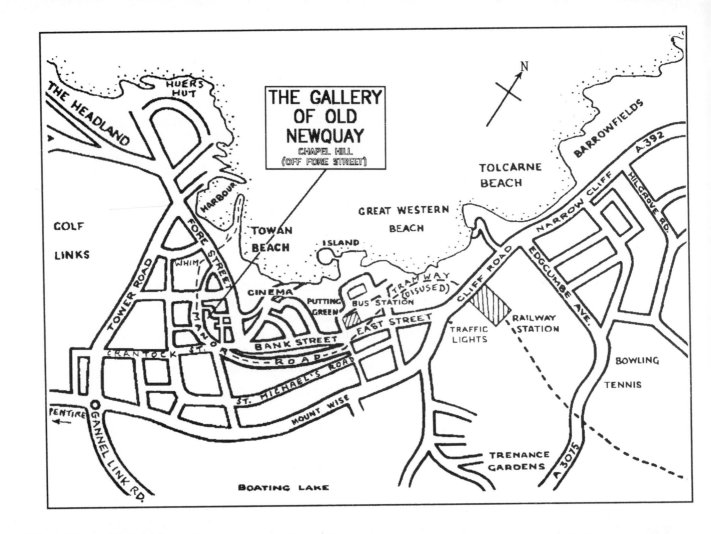

The original St Michael's Church or Chapel of Ease, the foundation stone of which was laid in March 1858. Demolished in 1938, it was situated on the site now occupied by Woolworth's.

A view from the top of Marcus Hill before the Atlantic Hotel was built in 1892.

Looking down Beach Road with Steps Malt House on the right. One of six malt houses in Newquay where barley was converted into malt for beer making.

At the bottom of the hill is Towan Promenade which was the site of a Mineral Water factory & Steam Laundry! The small low building on the left is a Refreshment Room.

Looking towards the Promenade with Speculation Fish Cellar, the long low building. Note lack of buildings on the Island. The boat is unloading cargo.

The Island quite bare and before the famous suspension bridge was built in 1900. Formerly known as Jago's Island where chickens were kept.

Bathing machines on Towan Beach.

The Donkeys' Parade on Towan beach in front of the then canvas and wood Cosy Nook Theatre. Its more substantial replacement was recently demolished.

The Harbour without the familiar Atlantic Hotel in the background. The boats took away mainly iron ore, china clay and grain. Incoming vessels brought coal, bone manure, limestone and salt (for salting the pilchards).

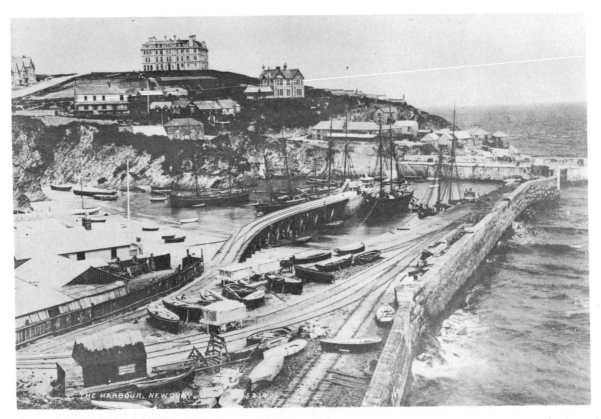

The Atlantic Hotel, opened in 1892, has now been built. The harbour is still a working one. The jetty in the centre was erected c. 1872 and its last load taken in 1926.

The harbour again, this time showing the lime kiln in the foreground. Limestone was imported and burnt in the kilns to make it suitable for use as fertilizer.

Behind the schooners one can see a paddle steamer, probably an excursion from South Wales via North Devon.

The fishing fleet is putting to sea. Note the length of the oars, used standing up, very similar to boats still in use in Portugal.

Active Cellar, above North Pier of the Harbour. A cellar had to be big enough to hold 500 hogs heads (barrels), each holding 2,500-3,000 pilchards. Nets etc. were stored in the loft above.

The fishermen associated with Unity Cellar.

'A bumper catch'.

The nearest hotel to the Harbour, known as Prouts. Now the Red Lion.

The 'Huers' were the men who kept watch for shoals of pilchards. When they sighted them the Huers raised the 'hue and cry' to the village below with the aid of their horns.

The Huer's Hut where the Huers could shelter. This may originally have been a hermitage. Its date is unknown but the windows suggest 14th century. It was restored in 1835 by a man named Vivian who was paid in fish.

Two of H.M. Coastguards together with an admirer. The coastguard lookout which, today, is under the War Memorial near the Atlantic Hotel. The memorial was unveiled in 1921 by H.R.H. the Prince of Wales.

The Lifeboat men of Newquay around 1910.

LAUNCHING THE LIFE BOAT, NEWQUAY.

Bringing the lifeboat to the slipway, which was the steepest in Britain, built in 1875 and improved in 1895. The lifeboat house and slipway can still be seen on the Headland today.

A practice launch on Lifeboat Day, usually August Bank Holiday.

Fistral Beach before the Golf Links was laid out in the 1890s. Note the low cliff, now covered by blown sand.

A rural scene overlooking Pentire Head. Sheep grazing on the headlands and adjoining sandy areas was a common sight at one time.

At the extreme point of East Pentire (from the Cornish pen = end, tyr = land). the remains of what must have been a fine barrow (Bronze-age burial site of about 1500 BC). Now worn down and defaced with a seat and notice board.

The Gannel (Crooked Estuary) looking upstream. This was one of the few navigable inlets on the North Cornish coast. Many lead and iron mines were worked in the area making this a much used waterway for the transportation of ore and other materials. Shipbuilding was also carried on here. Shipyards being worked from 1839-81.

Alas! These coastguard cottages in Fore Street built in 1825 are no longer with us. The site is now used as a car park. In the background is the old lifeboat house, now a shop.

Fore Street, Newquay

Fore Street looking towards Central Square.

Looking the other way from Central Square we have Jenkin's original premises before being rebuilt with a clock tower.

Commercial (now Central) Square decorated for the visit of the Prince and Princess of Wales in 1909. There was an inn on the site in 1755, but the age of the original building is unknown. At one time named the Dolphin, by 1837 it had become the Old Inn. It was rebuilt and reopened as the Commercial in 1859, became the Central Hotel in 1915, and has been the Central Inn since 1983.

Just off Central Square at the bottom of Crantock Street is the Salvation Army Hall. It was built as a Methodist Chapel in 1833 at a cost of £170. Known as John Cotton's Chapel after an important member of the congregation, it was built of cob with a thatched roof.

Bank Street, Newquay. (II.)

Bank Street with the Newquay Arms on the right. Built c. 1837 and rebuilt c. 1879 it was always the New Inn until renamed in 1965.

Bank Street, looking down towards Central Square. The Devon and Cornwall Bank on the right is now Trueform, and on the opposite corner is Dixon's.

A view from the same spot looking in the opposite direction. The tower of Wesley Church in centre of picture.

(above and facing page) Two views of the junction at the bottom of Marcus Hill, where horse-drawn wagons crossed the main street carrying china-clay etc. from the St. Austell area.

The house on the left in this photograph has been replaced by the bus station. The nearest building on the right housed one of the two town pumps - the other was at Central Square.

(above and facing page) The 'Whim' or winding engine situated behind Fore Street where the wagons were lowered to the Harbour down an inclined tunnel. The contents were then discharged into waiting ships for export. The Aquarium now stands in the entrance to the tunnel.

The original privately owned Information Bureau in Bank Street, photographed probably in the 1930s. It later became a shop.

Half way up East Street stands Wesley Church and this shows how the architect originally envisaged it, including a spire which was never built.

East Street looking towards Bank Street in 1900. Compare this with today's shops and restaurants!

Cliff Road before commercial interests changed its face. Stand with the Great Western Hotel on your right, and see the difference today.

Newquay 'Jingles' and the town porter outside the railway station.

The engine turntable in Cliff Road where shops now stand.

An excursion arriving. 1905.

A Motor-rail car on the Newquay-Chacewater line just before the war.

An early picture of the Great Western Hotel and neighbouring villas.

Views across Tolcarne Beach early 1930s. Note rows of bathing machines.

The promenade, now known as Narrowcliff, before extensions were made to all the private villas.

The same view in the 1920s.

Next we come to the public open space of Barrowfields. At its western end and overlooking Tolcarne Beach, is a large earthen mound with a prominent ditch. A very fine barrow - one of 15 which at one time occupied the site, a barrow or tumulus being a burial place of the Bronze Age.

If you walk to the end of Narrowcliff where Henver Road commences, you can see an old granite trough erected c. 1911 by the R.S.P.C.A. for watering horses.

Trevelgue Head or Porth Island is one of dozens of headlands around the Cornish coast known as 'cliff castles'. The name does not indicate a stone-built castle of Norman type but one used mainly by people of the Iron Age (in the case of Trevelgue 200 BC onwards). It was defended from the land by six ramparts and a chasm now crossed by a wooden bridge. Three of the ramparts are still clearly visible as we pass through them.

(above and facing page) Between Porth and St. Columb Minor along a footpath is a stile known as Burton's Stile. This commemorates the drunken progress of a commercial traveller of that name.

Porth Farm and Porth Way, both of which have been drastically altered. The former became the Chough public house between 1959 and the late 1980s.

Porth Beach, where the boat has probably been unloading coal. Ship building was carried on between 1818 and 1880.

A rural view of St. Columb Minor village and church. The church was built on partly Norman foundations c. 1417 and has the second highest tower in Cornwall, a noted landmark for Newquay and Padstow fishermen.

Church and shop at St. Columb Minor. In both these photographs the church has no clock. In 1910 money was donated for this purpose in memory of the Rev. Langford.

Trenance Valley from the Viaduct, Newquay.

Trenance Valley before the development of the lakes and gardens. Near the viaduct by the 'shrub basket' is a seat built of bricks made at Tolcarne Brickworks.

The Prince of Wales (in beret), later to become Edward VIII. Here he is inspecting the unemployed men who were transforming marshland into Trenance Lake in 1932. The worked on this job without pay apart from their dole money, but were given a hot meal each day and some tobacco. Their wives were given a packet of tea at the end of each week.

Trenance Viaduct carried what was at first an industrial tramway running from the clay district to Newquay Harbour. As our picture shows, it was of wooden trestle construction, later replaced by girders and in 1938, in anticipation of increased traffic, the present very pleasing arched viaduct was built.

A more recent picture showing Mellanvrane Mill. The wheel was fed by a leat which ran from the viaduct along the bottom of the gardens of the South side of the main road. A mill existed before 1775 when it belonged to Robert House and its last wheel was built c. 1870.

Not long after we pass the boating lake on the Crantock or Redruth road we pass over a concrete bridge. On the left is Trevemper Old Bridge, crossing the river Gannel. It is hard to believe that this bridge carried all east-bound traffic into Newquay, until 1924. It was rebuilt in the last century but a bridge is mentioned as early as 1613.

Trevemper Mill was shown on a map dated 1693. Demolished in 1964 after a fire in 1963. Henry Salmon 1914 was the last recorded miller.

AN IDEAL COMPANION TO THIS BOOK

AROUND NEWQUAY
by Bob Acton

Ten round walks in the Newquay area which focus on its rich and varied history. Frequent reference is made to photographs in "Newquay's Pictorial Past" in order to illustrate how much has changed.

In addition to walks in Newquay itself, the routes cover the coast from Bedruthan to Holywell, and inland walks include Trewerry Mill and the Tudor manor of Trerice, Colan church and Porth reservoir, St Columb Minor, and the beautiful Vale of Lanherne, which runs from St Columb Major via St Mawgan to the sea. The walks range from 2 to 10 miles in length, and shorter alternatives are given wherever possible.

AROUND NEWQUAY includes sketch maps, drawings and old photographs. Very detailed directions are given, together with advice on parking, availability of refreshments and other practical points.

The new edition of AROUND NEWQUAY, updated and greatly enlarged, is available now in local shops, Tourist Information Centres and at the Gallery of Old Newquay, price £3.30.